I0868003

SAINT JOSEPH

SAINT JOSEPH

TRUSTING GOD

Margarita Saldaña Mostajo

Paulist Press
New York / Mahwah, NJ

Unless otherwise stated, Scripture quotations are from the New Revised Standard Version Bible, copyright © 1989 National Council of the Churches of Christ in the United States of America. Used by permission. All rights reserved worldwide.

Cover image: *St. Joseph and the Christ Child,* 1955, Costantino Institute, Mirano (Venice)
Cover design by Joe Gallagher
Book design by Lynn Else

This book was originally published under the title: *San José: Los ojos de las entrañas* © Editorial Sal Terrae 2021 - Grupo de Comunicación Loyola, S. L. U. - Bilbao (Spain), gcloyola.com
+ The original book had an imprimatur by Manuel Sánchez Monge, Bishop of Santander (Spain)

Translated from Spanish by Luz M. Ibarra

Library of Congress Cataloging-in-Publication Data
Names: Saldaña Mostajo, Margarita, 1972- author.
Title: Saint Joseph : trusting God / Margarita Saldaña Mostajo.
Other titles: San José. English
Description: New York / Mahwah, NJ : Paulist Press, 2023.
Identifiers: LCCN 2022029918 (print) | LCCN 2022029919 (ebook) | ISBN 9780809155934 (paperback) | ISBN 9781587689956 (ebook)
Subjects: LCSH: Joseph, Saint.
Classification: LCC BS2458 .S3513 2023 (print) | LCC BS2458 (ebook) | DDC 232.9/32—dc23/eng/20220916
LC record available at https://lccn.loc.gov/2022029918
LC ebook record available at https://lccn.loc.gov/2022029919

ISBN 978-0-8091-5593-4 (paperback)
ISBN 978-1-58768-995-6 (e-book)

Published by Paulist Press
997 Macarthur Boulevard
Mahwah, New Jersey 07430
www.paulistpress.com

Printed and bound in the
United States of America

To my father,
Friend of Saint Joseph.
To Teresa and Engracia,
his daughters.

I will learn from you to be silent,
to pass dark on the earth,
like a traveler at night.

—Charles de Foucauld

TABLE OF CONTENTS

A LIFE WITHOUT A TABLE OF CONTENTS

Some time ago, a friend translated a manuscript into French and she forgot a small detail. When I sent it to another friend to review it, she replied to me by email: "Where is the table of contents? I can't find it anywhere, not at the beginning, not at the end!" She felt lost by not having the outline in advance and not being able to immediately locate chapters and pages.

In my eyes, this scene came to evoke our need to control reality in its minor details. It made me think that despite our expectations, every human life is a narrative that is always unfinished. It is a story whose plot is more or less unpredictable. It is a unique copy that opens with docility and joy before certain people, while it remains hermetically closed to the gaze of others. Through this reflection I began to have the intuition that the trajectory of Joseph of Nazareth also represents one of those particularly complex stories. It is constructed based on names, exposed to all sorts of ups and downs, woven of pains and joys and unexpected sources of everyday miracles.

Joseph's life, a life without a table of contents, may in the background look a lot like ours. It seems gray and insignificant most of the days, and at the same time, essential in the multicolored tapestry of the history of salvation. It seems insecure, with no paths laid out, but solidly established in the trust of a Presence that envelops everything. To read the depth of a text barely written in words, an external and superficial look is not enough. What is missing is an inner and penetrating gaze, first collected inward to contemplate in silence the mystery that moves existence, then poured out into the world to face reality from the perceived mystery.

I wish this book had no table of contents. Joseph, the protagonist, perhaps in spite of himself, invites us to leave known references and be guided by intuition. He also invites us not to plunge into formless chaos but to hear how this intuition resonates in our own hearts the rhythm that God was marking in his. Joseph teaches us how to close our eyes and open them in a different way...with the eyes of the heart.

Invoked for centuries as protector and guide, even today Joseph keeps a precious message, good news for our weary and suffering world. It seems no accident that Pope Francis wanted to dedicate the year of 2021 to Joseph, a year born shaken by the pandemic.

It has been a time without a table of contents, like the life of Joseph, who gives himself to our inner gaze to be assumed in his contradictions, cradled in his frailties, recreated with tenderness and audacity in its unprecedented possibilities.

NAMES

"MAY GOD ADD"

One's name has supreme importance in the existence of a person. In the biblical world, a name sometimes expresses the mission of the recipient, as in the case of Jesus: "God saves." At other times, it indicates a radical transformation: "No longer shall your name be Abram, but your name shall be Abraham; for I have made you the ancestor of a multitude of nations" (Gen 17:5).

Joseph of Nazareth, a pious Jew, certainly knew the roots of his own name, that of one of the twelve patriarchs of Israel. That Joseph of the Old Testament was born after his mother went through a painful experience of sterility. Rachel, like so many other women throughout Scripture, lives for years confronted with disgraces. She fails to gain social recognition, being unable to perform as a mother and to bear children for her husband, Jacob.

Joseph's birth happens later, after Jacob has already had ten sons and one daughter! Some were with his first wife, Leah, and others with two slaves, Bilhah and Zilpah. "Then God remembered Rachel. God heeded her and opened her womb. She conceived and bore a son, and said, 'God has taken away my reproach.' She named him Joseph, saying, 'May the Lord add to me another son!'" (Gen 30:22–24).

By the simple fact of existing, Joseph allows a full life for a woman, his own mother, whose sterility had so far prevented her from completely finding her place in the community. Through Joseph, God removes the outrage that tortured Rachel. At the same time, this child widens the nurturing desire of his mother, who invokes God pleading, "May the Lord add another child." The name of Joseph then contains a desire for abundance, for multiplication. Joseph: May the Lord add.

The Book of Genesis continues to narrate how this wish will come true; it will be fulfilled in due time, but by surely different paths from those that Rachel would have imagined: "Then they journeyed from Bethel; and when they were still some distance from Ephrath, Rachel was in childbirth, and she had hard labor. When she was in her hard labor, the midwife said to her, 'Do not be afraid; for now you will have another son.' As her soul was departing (for she died), she named him Ben-oni [son of my pain]. But his father called him Benjamin [son of good omen]. So Rachel died, and she was buried on the way to Ephrath (that is, Bethlehem)" (Gen 35:16–19) [NRSV translation, slightly modified].

Rachel, the mother of the patriarch Joseph, dies in Bethlehem giving birth to her last son, Benjamin. The life of this child takes her own life, while fulfilling the desire for fertility that has shaped and guided her entire existence. The biblical author emphasizes that God always performs as promised, adding and multiplying, although his plans do not unfold exactly as human beings could hope. Benjamin, the "son of pain," paradoxically becomes a "son of good omen."

Joseph of Nazareth, without choosing it, receives a difficult name. He is called to allow God to constantly add new chapters to the plot of his life, not counting on a previous script that allows him to screen what would suit him best personally. He is invited in deep freedom and trust to consent without arguing. He is almost pushed to the edge and that implies being guided by circumstances that end up generating good outcomes, but that in their origins show nothing but risk and disadvantage. With this attitude, Joseph allows God to add. With his determination, Joseph himself adds the possibility of realization to the dreams of God.

DREAMER

If the Christian tradition has not paid great attention to the origins of the name of Joseph, it has developed on the contrary, a splendid parallelism between the adult life of the patriarch and the figure of the earthly father of Jesus. Both of them have dreams that tremendously complicate their life. They both know danger and uncertainty and they both come to Egypt by providential circumstances. Joseph was born during Jacob's old age and he was the favorite of his father. He dreamed frequently. The rest of his brothers envied him and conspired against him. "They said to one another, 'Here comes the dreamer. Come now, let us kill him and throw him into one of the pits; then we shall say that a wild animal has devoured him, and we shall see what will become of his dreams'" (Gen 37:19–20).

The rest of the story is very familiar to us. Joseph arrives in Egypt apparently by chance, sold by his brothers to some merchants who were heading there. In the midst of strangers, the dreamer despised in his own house can now display his gift of dream interpretation. Thanks to this he earns credibility with Pharaoh and he is appointed prime minister. In the time of famine, Joseph administers the granaries of Egypt with wisdom and with the authority received from Pharaoh: "Go to Joseph, what he says to you, do" (Gen 41:55).

Later this privileged situation will allow him to help his brothers, first with great discretion and later openly, having forgiven from the heart all the evil received: "I am your brother Joseph, whom you sold into Egypt. And now do not be distressed, or angry with yourselves, because you sold me here; for God sent me before you to preserve life" (Gen 45:4–5). For those who open themselves to the action of grace, past wounds become a source of life and dreams are transformed into very tangible realities.

"As he had done with Mary, God revealed his saving plan to Joseph. He did so by using dreams, which in the Bible and among all ancient peoples were considered a way for him to make his will known" (Pope Francis, *Patris Corde* 3). In His infinite creativity, God finds multiple ways to provide each person with certain "clues" that point toward orienting life within God's will. God seems to use very different language with Mary and with Joseph, despite both being called to intimately link their destinies toward the plan of salvation.

According to Luke, Mary receives a visit from the archangel Gabriel, a messenger of God who has his own name. Nothing allows us to think that she is asleep—everything is otherwise. A personal dialogue takes place between the young woman and the angel, a brief but rich interaction in the details given. Mary has the chance to ask and express her consent. Words of consolation that comfort and encourage float through the air: "Greetings, favored one! The Lord is with you....Do not be afraid, Mary, for you have found favor with God....He will reign over the house of Jacob forever, and of his kingdom there will no end....Nothing is impossible for God" (Luke 1:28, 30, 33, 37).

The revelation that Joseph receives is no less true, although God chooses to communicate with him in a language stripped down with surprising sobriety. Joseph, like Mary, is also visited by "the angel of the Lord." But here it is with an anonymous messenger with whom he will not be able to establish any kind of dialogue. Joseph is asleep, in a state of passivity.

The content of his dreams–four, according to Matthew–go strictly to the essentials. In the first of them, Joseph understands that he cannot disown Mary because she has conceived of the Holy Spirit a son who will save the people from their sins, and whose name will be Jesus. The other dreams contain nothing but direct orders: "Get up... Run away... Stay there... on the way...." Joseph is not offered the possibility to formulate questions or to negotiate. The words are neither reassuring nor confirming, except for a "fear not" in the first of his dreams.

With each new announcement and each step "added," Joseph welcomes it with his eyes closed. He's not just asleep. He is allowing his inner energies to concentrate in order to carry the burden of a story that occurs and to which he wishes to hold fast with all his heart, with all of his mind, with all of his soul, with all of his strength. With the eyes of the heart wide open, Joseph contemplates how a new *šhema'* begins to be written in the heart of history. "You shall love the Lord your God": the nucleus of the law and of the prophets begins to acquire perplexing meaning to him.

Those eyes of the heart, deeply directed toward the contemplation of the essential in the midst of the confusion of dreams, give Joseph a capacity unheard of to interpret reality and to take over. When he wakes up, the full movement of his existence expresses perhaps better than any word his commitment to the message received: "When Joseph awoke from sleep, he did as the angel of the Lord commanded him" (Matt 1:24).

HUSBAND OF MARY

Curiously, Joseph is a male whose appearance in the biblical text seems justified in the first place by the existence of a woman. His quality of "husband of Mary" gives him a place in the genealogies of Matthew and arouses the interest of Luke, who portrays him going from Nazareth to Bethlehem to register, according to the order by Caesar Augustus.

The Evangelists accurately point out that Mary was "young," while Elizabeth, Zechariah, and the prophetess Ana were "of advanced age." Tradition has attributed to Simeon the nickname "old man";

his prayer leads us to conclude that at the time of the birth of Jesus this "just and pious" man was already near to his death: "Master, now you are dismissing your servant in peace, according to your word; for my eyes have seen your salvation" (Luke 2:29–30).

That same tradition, and in a particular way the iconography, wanted to see an old man in Joseph too, although biblical data does not legitimize such a representation. Similarly in Matthew as in Luke, the figure of Joseph disappears completely from the scene at the end of Jesus' childhood. This could be considered as an indication that he has died. Even if we admit such a hypothesis, given the short life expectancy in the ancient world, dying would not be the same as aging earlier.

On the other hand, it is meaningful that during Jesus' ministry he is recognized as the son of Joseph, a character who is still alive at least in the memory of the Lord's contemporaries: "Is not this Jesus, the son of Joseph, whose father and mother we know?" (John 6:42), the astonished Jews ask themselves in Capernaum after Jesus had claimed to be the bread that came down from heaven. The people of Nazareth show the same skepticism when Jesus returns to his hometown and begins to teach in the synagogue: "Where did this man get this wisdom and the deeds of powers? Is not this the carpenter's son?" (Matt 13:54–55).

The question, then, is where did the desire to turn Joseph into an elderly husband come from? An initial way to respond may come from the need to explain the existence of certain "brothers and sisters of Jesus," attested by Mark 6:3 and Matthew 13:55. Some Fathers of the Greek and Latin Church, as well as the apocryphal Gospels, support the idea that these relatives (considered by some ancient authors as blood brothers and by others as cousins) were actually stepbrothers of Jesus, children that Joseph fathered in a first marriage. According to this view, Joseph would have been married to Mary when he was older.

The explanation can also be found with the purpose of justifying the perpetual virginity of Mary. Matthew states that Joseph "took her as his wife, but had no marital relations with her until she had borne a son; and he named him Jesus" (Matt 1:25). The Evangelist here uses the term *to know* in the semitic sense to maintain marital relations and in no way comments on what could have happened after the birth. Luke uses the same verb in chapter one, when Mary answers the angel: "But how can this come about, since I have no knowledge of man? (Luke 1:34, NJB).

From these texts, tradition concludes that Mary was always a virgin, as it was affirmed at the Second Council of Constantinople (AD 553): "If anyone calls the saint glorious always Virgin Mary mother of God, in a figurative sense and not in a proper sense..., let it be anathema" (Denzinger, *Enchiridion*, 427). Mary "always Virgin" would have specially needed a virtuous husband by her side; hence it becomes a certain advantage that Joseph is not in the prime of his life. The lily flower, a sign of purity, will easily become one of the iconographic symbols of that saint.

Beyond the controversial nature of certain texts or affirmations, it is really interesting to consider that Joseph and Mary form a true human couple. Together, they must learn to build the codes of their relationship. Such codes are evidently determined by their social, cultural, and religious settings.

In the Jewish world at the time of Jesus, monogamous marriage follows the betrothal contract made from age eighteen for males and age twelve for women. From that moment, the male becomes head of household and assumes responsibility to support the offspring, ensuring a livelihood and respect for the law. The woman is expected to have and raise children, while being subordinate to her husband.

At the time of the annunciation, Joseph and Mary already have committed themselves through betrothal to reciprocal fidelity. With their unexpected plans, God "adds" a good dose of instability to what their relationship is supposed to be. Mary goes to Elizabeth's house for three months, having to avoid the dangers for a woman who is not traveling with her husband. Joseph let her go, without holding her back, without trying to keep her from offering the world all the love she is capable of giving.

Surely worried by the anticipation of this journey, Joseph looks once more inwardly and contemplates internally the freedom of Mary. When he opens his eyes again, perhaps he encourages her to get on her way, to hug Elizabeth, and to let her song flow. He also may exclaim with joy: "My soul magnifies the Lord, and my spirit rejoices in God my Savior" (Luke 1:46–47).

The essence of chaste love between Mary and Joseph is found precisely here, in the freedom with which both are able to relate to one another and to open up to others. When commenting on the term "most chaste" that tradition has attributed to Joseph, Pope Francis enlarges a vision that has been often too narrow:

> That title is not simply a sign of affection, but the summation of an attitude that is the opposite of possessiveness. Chastity is freedom from possessiveness in every sphere of one's life. Only when love is chaste is it truly love. A possessive love ultimately becomes dangerous: it imprisons, constricts, and makes for misery. God himself loved humanity with a chaste love. He left us free even to go astray and set ourselves against him. The logic of love is always the logic of freedom, and Joseph knew how to love with extraordinary freedom. He never made himself the center of things. He did not

think of himself but focused instead on the lives of Mary and Jesus. (Pope Francis, *Patris Corde* 7)

JUST

Another of the titles that Matthew grants to Joseph and that the Christian people have preserved with eagerness, is that of "just." After introducing him as the "husband of Mary," the Evangelist affirms: "Her husband, Joseph, being a righteous man and unwilling to expose her to public disgrace, planned to dismiss her quietly" (Matt 1:19).

In the Mediterranean basin of the first century there were several notions of justice. The Empire enforced the Roman justice, which advocated giving each one what is right. The allegorical image of this concept is a blindfolded woman, representing justice, holding in her hand a scale that indicates equity. In Palestine at the same time, the Mosaic justice ruled.

If Joseph had followed justice literally, he should have abandoned Mary in public. That was what "justice" obligated him to do, with or without the announcement of the angel, only by the fact she was carrying in her womb a son who was not Joseph's. In that case, Mary would have been considered adulterous and subjected to being stoned.

However, Joseph uses another criterion of justice anchored in biblical tradition. He knows that the God of Israel shows justice in the capacity to have mercy, and in that case, restoring the balance of the scale for justice means inclining it in favor of the weakest. God is not blindfolded in order to be impartial but rather precisely avoids neutrality and seeks how to help those who need it the most.

Joseph's justice is a human virtue that has already been developed in him before receiving the message from God. It is conceivable that his own path—of which we know almost nothing—involving daily respect for the law, relationships he has established over time..., all this has been developing his capacity to be just. This justice is revealed in his way of making a serious and painful decision. Joseph ignores what has happened when Mary is found pregnant. But he considers her to be "the weaker part" and he is in support of her. Matthew doesn't stop to analyze Joseph's feelings. He only says that "he did not want to expose her." Beyond what has happened, regardless of the guilt or innocence of Mary, Joseph "does not want" to expose her and so consequently he decides to secretly repudiate her:

> Joseph accepted Mary unconditionally. He trusted in the angel's words. The nobility of Joseph's heart is such that what he learned from the law he made dependent on charity. Today, in our world where psychological, verbal, and physical violence toward women is so evident,

> Joseph appears as the figure of a respectful and sensitive man. Even though he does not understand the bigger picture, he makes a decision to protect Mary's good name, her dignity, and her life. In his hesitation about how best to act, God helped him by enlightening his judgment. (Pope Francis, *Patris Corde* 4)

Once again, Joseph looks at the outer reality with the eyes of the heart and lets himself be moved, perhaps where his emotional wounds suggested acting differently.

Without knowing, Joseph becomes a precursor of justice from the kingdom that Jesus will preach much later. He is perhaps the first of those "merciful" ones of the New Testament that have "hunger and thirst for uprightness" (cf. Matt 5:6–7). He will find his own happiness by choosing Mary, faithful to his consciousness, perhaps regardless of the advice of some "wise and intelligent." At his side, Jesus might well learn that only a kind of justice that exceeds that of the scribes and the Pharisees is able to open the door of a kingdom where only the little ones find a place.

FATHER OF JESUS

Mark does not attribute to Jesus another father other than God, and with this affirmation he begins his Gospel (cf. Mark 1:1). The other two synoptics (cf. Matt 13:55 and Luke 2:48), as well as John (see John 6:42), refer to Joseph as "father," recognizing Jesus as his son or "son of the carpenter." The tradition will be forced to make a distinction of this powerful title and to declare two important facts: the divinity of Jesus whose "true Father" is God and the Immaculate Conception. In order to dare to talk about Joseph as a father, the coming centuries will add some adjectives, such as adoptive father, legal father, nurturing father:

> Fathers are not born but made. A man does not become a father simply by bringing a child into the world, but by taking up the responsibility to care for that child. Whenever a man accepts responsibility for the life of another, in some way he becomes a father to that person. (Pope Francis, *Patris Corde* 7)

If we pay attention to the pope, we have to affirm that Joseph is also the "true father" of Jesus. The paternity—and maternity, we must say—implies more than mere begetting. Conceiving a son is a short process; building a maternal or paternal relationship is a task of a lifetime.

A first attribute of Joseph's paternity, Pope Francis emphasizes, consists of the integrity of his responsibility. When he assumes Jesus as his son, he does so fully and unconditionally. He no longer looks back or murmurs objections when the situation gets complicated. Joseph will answer for the life of Jesus as far as it is necessary. According to Matthew, by preserving the integrity of the child he will be able to undertake a long and uncertain road to Egypt and search, in an unknown environment, for the way to obtain bread for the family.

The tradition in Saint Luke omits the episode of the flight to Egypt. But this Evangelist also confirms Joseph's responsibility in echoing his anguish when Jesus stays in the Temple of Jerusalem without notifying his parents. This pilgrimage closes with a verse full of content: "He went down with them and came to Nazareth, and he lived under their authority" (Luke 2:51). Jesus, a teenager, establishes a dependent and obedient relationship with his parents, like any person of his age would do. Joseph, therefore, practices the role of being a father.

With Mary, Joseph is deeply committed to the education of Jesus, helping him to become the exceptional man he will be one day. Joseph saw Jesus progress day by day "in wisdom and in years, and in divine and human favor" (Luke 2:52). As the Lord did with Israel, "so he taught him to walk, took him in his arms...[as] a father for him who raises a boy up to his cheeks, and leans toward him to feed him" (cf. Hos 11: 3–4). Jesus saw the tenderness of God in Joseph: "As a father has compassion for his children, so the

Lord has compassion for those who fear him (Ps 103:13)" (Pope Francis, *Patris Corde* 2).

The Aramaic term *abba* is used in a familiar sense for children to call their parents. Jesus must have learned it from Mary's lips to address Joseph. This man was for him a true father, a "dad," and through his face Jesus was discovering the characteristics of his own Abba. As a male, Joseph was also a model of masculine identification for Jesus. The way Jesus related to women and the deep freedom and delicacy in evidence during his ministry may well have been learned from the figure of his father and in seeing the relationship Joseph established with Mary.

In the family circle first and in the public space later, Joseph is a true teacher of Jesus. If Mary, like so many other mothers, teaches her son to talk and walk, Joseph takes him to the synagogue, sharing with him the foundations of Israel's faith, and introduces him to the occupation of carpenter. Many attitudes of Jesus were shaped in having daily contact with his father: attention to small things, capacity for wonder, patience, prudence, absolute generosity up to the extreme of giving his own life for all.

Over the years, Joseph faithfully carries out the commitment that the angel entrusted to him in dreams: "Take the child and his mother." He is not merely receiving Mary, adopting Jesus, and acting as legal father. His material care, his presence, and his testimony allow God to enhance his plans with ease.

Joseph anticipates the new relationships of the kingdom, which are not based on blood ties but on the ties between all those who truly seek God and want to do the heavenly Father's will.

FATHER OF THE POOR

Popular piety invokes Joseph with devotion as "father of the poor." The images of him with the Baby Jesus in his arms have occupied many homes of modest people. Countless saints have him as a privileged companion to whom they attribute their receiving special help in desperate situations. The great Teresa of Jesus will affirm:

> I took for my advocate and lord the glorious Saint Joseph and commended myself earnestly to him; and I found that this my father and lord delivered me both from this trouble and also from other and greater troubles concerning my honor and the loss of my soul, and that he gave me greater blessings than I could ask of him. I do not remember even now that I have ever asked anything of him which he has failed to grant. (Teresa of Avila, *Life* 6:6)

Joseph can come to the aid of poor people because he has known poverty in his own flesh and because he has broadened his stores of mercy to share with others. "It was not the rich who frequently called the carpenter of Nazareth at the door: guests who arrived were poor," said Charles de Foucauld in 1897, after having contemplated many times the figure of Joseph.

Joseph has experienced what it means to make uncomfortable and dangerous journeys, as well as how to take care of a pregnant woman or a newborn. He knows what it is like to suffer from not finding a better place to lay a baby than in a manger. He understands what it is like to accompany Mary at the temple for her purification, carrying the offering of a poor person—a pair of turtledoves or two pigeons—while wealthy women look at them over their shoulders offering a one-year-old lamb (cf. Lev 12:6–8). He is aware, however, that there are other less fortunate people, who only manage to offer a little fine flour (cf. Lev 5:11).

Joseph also knows the poverty of having to emigrate against his own expectations. He has to face the lack of balance to enter an unknown land. He feels the distrustful glance from those who treat him as a foreigner. He does not know their tongue and must overcome the difficulty of understanding others and being understood himself. He urgently needs a source of income and he has his own skillful hands, it is true. But they are foreigners' hands that nobody easily trusts. He lacks credentials; he simply has no papers in Egypt.

When he returns to Nazareth, Joseph faces a changed a reality, with things not exactly as he had left them years ago. Meanwhile, he has lost his customers and has to start from scratch. He does not even know if his house has been occupied by others. The Nazarenes suspiciously observe a neighbor who went away without saying goodbye and now he returns, as if nothing happened.

In another sense, Joseph lives the radical poverty of the deep loneliness: who will believe that God has spoken to him in dreams? Who can tell the secret of their going and coming? Who—but Mary—could understand that Jesus is his son, in a completely different way than others in Israel would imagine?...Joseph goes through the poverty of silence, not because he does not have anything to say, but because he lacks suitable interlocutors to embrace this mystery.

Christians have discovered the deep capacity of Joseph's empathy, born of knowing that he can from his own experience accompany those who suffer. No pain is unknown to him, whether material poverty, spiritual darkness, anguish, doubts, fear...

Finally, Joseph has lived to the extreme the essence from Matthew 25. He fed Jesus when he was hungry and spared no effort to find water in the midst of walks and fatigue. He worked to dress him and put shoes on him, so that he would lack for nothing essential. He taught him everything within his reach: how to relate to people, learn a trade, and earn a living. He also taught him to dream, to close his eyes and look at reality from the inside out, to open them later and enter temporal existence with determination. Joseph cared for Jesus if he was ever sick. He protected him while they were immigrants. He accompanied his growth and stimulated his capabilities. He respected his disagreements. He knew how to let him be himself.

Perhaps for these few reasons and many others,

> Every poor, needy, suffering or dying person, every stranger, every prisoner, every infirm person is "the child" whom Joseph continues to protect. For this reason, Saint Joseph is invoked as protector of people who are unfortunate, needy, exiled, afflicted, poor, and dying in their poverty. Consequently, the Church cannot fail to show a special love for the least of our brothers and sisters, for Jesus showed a particular concern for them and personally identified with them. (Pope Francis, *Patris Corde* 5)

Let's dream with Joseph....Let's dream of a poor Church and a Church for poor people....Joseph will also be her protector, he who was officially appointed patron of the Catholic Church by Pius IX in 1870:

> God trusted Joseph, as did Mary, who found in him someone who would not only save her life but would always provide for her and her child. In this sense, Saint Joseph could not be

other than the Guardian of the Church, for the Church is the continuation of the Body of Christ in history. (Pope Francis, *Patris Corde* 5)

PROTECTOR OF THE WORKERS

"There is no poverty worse than that which takes away work and the dignity of work." In a genuinely developed society, work is an essential dimension of social life, for it is not only a means of earning one's daily bread, but also of personal growth, the building of healthy relationships, self-expression, and the exchange of gifts. Work gives us a sense of shared responsibility for the development of the world, and ultimately, for our life as a people. (Pope Francis, *Fratelli Tutti* 162)

During the Industrial Revolution in the nineteenth century, people's awareness grew of shameful injustices workers suffered, subjected to subhuman living conditions, with exhausting working hours and inadequate remuneration to have a dignified existence. Revolutionary movements led the fight for a structural transformation of the workers' world. During this process, many Christians left the Church, instead finding answers to their real needs outside the traditional Catholic rhetoric.

Pope Leo XIII, with his encyclical *Rerum Novarum* (1893), timidly began to raise the voice of the magisterium. He denounced disgraceful environments, unjust wages, and other severe attacks against the workers' dignity. However, not even the pontiff's social thought, nor huge pastoral efforts like the one of the Jesuit Francisco Butiñá, accompanied by women like Isabel de Marangues or Bonifacia Rodríguez, managed to stop the secularization of the world of work. In the background, the Church spent a long time trying to harmonize incompatible extremes; poor people, assisted by her with constant care, did not always find in her proposals a valid reason to fight for their dignity.

In 1955, Pius XII declared Saint Joseph the patron of workers. His feast, established on May 1, brought a trace of Catholic influence to commemoration of International Labor Day, a traditional domain of the left. Considering the type of worker Joseph could have been helps those people who earn their living by the sweat of their brow, that they may find in him a true protector these two thousand years later.

According to Pope Francis, "Saint Joseph was a carpenter who earned an honest living to provide for his family. From him, Jesus learned the value, the dignity, and the joy of what it means to eat bread that is the fruit of one's own labor" (Pope Francis, *Patris Corde* 6). Certainly...but let's go a little further.

"Is not this the carpenter's son?" (Matt 13:55), the crowds wondered in amazement one day when he was teaching in the synagogue of Nazareth. We know that the father, the carpenter, was Joseph. Both Matthew and Mark use a precise Greek term to indicate the office of Joseph and later of Jesus: *téktōn*, meaning craftsman. At that time, this word did not indicate the concept of the word carpenter we use today, a worker self-employed who manages his own workshop. Joseph was *téktōn*, that is, someone who was engaged in construction in projects of greater or lesser importance and working with materials such as iron, stone, and wood.

The Gospels do not mention any "Nazareth workshop." This representation, which is very well known, prevents us from seeing Saint Joseph doing small jobs for someone else. The fact of having a trade to earn a living and technical knowledge indicates that Joseph was not among the poorest of his hometown. However, let us not forget that the social organization of Palestine in the first century is like a pyramid, the top of which represents a minority of rich people, while the rest of the population struggles to survive. Joseph and his family are "one of many" in that mass of human beings.

We understand better from these considerations why Joseph can be seen as the protector of workers. To begin with, he knows the hardness of manual labor, which leaves marks on his own body: sweat, calluses, fatigue....Joseph knows what form of prayer is capable of inhabiting an exhausted body and he understands the absences and "negligence" often caused by exhausting hours. Joseph knows the uncertainty of going out to look for a job without knowing if he will find it. He knows the anguish of coming back home with nothing in his pocket. He learns to trust in the providence of God who cares for poor people. Joseph has suffered the tax burden and the injustice that oppresses the little ones, ruined with few resources while the rich live comfortably on their income. Then Joseph can understand the indignation of those who call for a fairer order and of those who organize to make it come true.

Tradition has rightly emphasized that Jesus learned from Joseph's side the honesty and joy for a job well done, the greatness of going on creating the world side by side with God. Joseph will have closed his eyes many times to stare in grateful wonder at the beauty and usefulness of the works born from his own hands. Then, with his eyes wide open, Joseph will have taught Jesus that the world is broken by injustice and that poor people are constantly wounded in their dignity as daughters and sons, as sisters and brothers. Joseph may have told Jesus that God still needs skillful hands to mend the cracks of a suffering humanity; suffering and warm hands to anoint the world with the balm of tenderness.

Next to Joseph, workers of all times can sharpen the eyes of their own hearts, shake hands, and find a safe companion on their long road of searching.

PAINS AND JOYS

It is no secret to anyone that our existence is full of pains and joys. There's no use trying to run away from what hurts in order to take refuge in happy moments. These moments exist, certainly, but they do not last forever. When we pretend to capture them, they evaporate and leave us with a bitter feeling, as if happiness were a right, as if they owe us joy.

The art of life consists perhaps in letting go of excessive expectations to match the circumstances with the confidence that, in the midst of what might happen, God wants and can come to meet us. Nothing is further from the optimistic illusion that "everything is going to be fine."

When the COVID-19 pandemic struck in early 2020, a microscopic virus violently unmasked this deception and today we feel we know practically nothing. The absence of our loved ones afflicted and hurt us. We were afraid of the future and of having lost forever what we once considered "normal." We were mired in uncertainty, which included our ability to project ourselves forward. A certain apprehension settled into our relationships and way of living, and sometimes we were distressed by not knowing whether we were acting correctly amid the dangers.

The situation has been so surprising, so unstable, and so changing that it has produced great misunderstanding. Previously unheard-of barriers have been raised in how we treat each other: forbidden to cross certain boundaries and enter the houses of others; forbidden to approach, touch, see one another's face, give each other a hug. Neither the politicians nor scientists managed to readily solve this planetary crisis: what a disappointment.

Believers are not spared even a miniscule amount of being human; the only advantage we have is the ability the Spirit impresses within us to keep walking like everyone else and with an attitude of hope, with a glance of confidence. The lives of the saints, those models proposed by the Church, allow us to see how they faced difficulties of all kinds. Their holiness does not lie in perfection but in the ongoing desire of living dark moments embraced by God; faith, hope and love are the key.

In this sense, Joseph's life is no different from other saints' paths nor ours. Even though he did not know the COVID-19 pandemic, as we do, he did not lack crises and difficulties that tested his ability to believe, hope, and love. Like us, Joseph did not find immediate answers to every question he had. This is a process. In every event through which he lived, Joseph stumbled with resistance and limitations. He experienced severe pain but did not shut himself up or stop there. Where some would say, "Enough," the believer whispers, "Let it be done." In that always unfinished process, pains and joys are intertwined in the unfolding history of salvation.

FROM DISAPPOINTMENT TO EMBRACE

> Her husband Joseph, being a righteous man and unwilling to expose her to public disgrace, planned to dismiss her quietly. But just when he had resolved to do this, an angel of the Lord appeared to him in a dream and said, "Joseph, son of David, do not be afraid to take Mary as your wife, for the child conceived in her is from the Holy Spirit...." When Joseph awoke from sleep, he did as the angel of the Lord commanded him; he took her as his wife. (Matt 1:19–20, 24)

Disappointment is one of the most painful experiences in human relationships. While we are angry with someone, there is still a possibility of arguing and clearing things up. Disappointment, on the other hand, runs the risk of putting a final point, making us feel that it is no longer worth moving on. When someone expresses that we have disappointed him, it is as if deep down he said, "Whatever you do, whatever you say, I can't go on believing in you." Disappointment has killing power.

How many times in the face of a disappointment, we allow our wounded ego to take charge of our decisions that follow. Pain blurs and clouds our sight, like a spreading oil stain in a tablecloth. In this way, it is impossible to reason with good sense, open ourselves to listening to the other, and perhaps consider aspects of the issue that go unnoticed. We start looking at the person who has let us down from that single crystal, unfairly reducing her and depriving her of any possibility for the future.

The incarnation of the Son of God also brings the human experience of disappointment. Although the Evangelists do not describe Joseph's feelings, it seems reasonable that he feels disappointed in Mary. The woman he loves and the one he trusts, the woman he's engaged to is expecting a child from another father. If we put ourselves in Joseph's skin, it's hard to imagine anything more than pain and disappointment:

> Often in life, things happen whose meaning we do not understand. Our first reaction is frequently one of disappointment and rebellion.

> Joseph set aside his own ideas in order to accept the course of events and, mysterious as they seemed, to embrace them, take responsibility for them, and make them part of his own history. Unless we are reconciled with our own history, we will be unable to take a single step forward, for we will always remain hostage to our expectations and the disappointments that follow. (Pope Francis, *Patris Corde* 4)

The interesting thing about Joseph's reaction is that he does not remain locked in his feelings nor allow himself to be dominated by his naturally wounded male ego. His love for Mary is much greater than the current disappointment. That love allows him, despite the pain, to start a process of reconciliation within himself and with her as well. Joseph does not understand and accepts that he does not understand. But he does not inwardly seek revenge. Before the angel gives him some explanation, he has already made his plans—to dismiss Mary secretly—without falling into the trap of freely doing evil. Joseph respects himself and he decides not to marry Mary, at the same time he is offering her a way out for her life to go on.

This attitude in Joseph encourages him to walk the path that goes from disappointment to embrace. Receiving Mary in his house is an authentic gesture, a source no doubt of infinite joy for both. We cannot embrace once more the one who has let us down if we do not give her trust in return, if not absolute—because history leaves traces—at least enough. Where there is no embrace and reconciliation all sores rot and life is extinguished.

Some life stories, however, find no other destiny than to be separated. Certain wounds, in order to heal, require distance. This happens in all areas of life: relationships, friendship, community relations, labor relations....Even when someone has to depart, it is possible to leave and to embrace one whom we have disappointed or who has disappointed us. Aware that we cannot comprehend all the factors and that each person bears part of the responsibility, we wish the person well and let him or her go from our life, allowing for their continuing and new future. Going from disappointment to embrace is not impossible. Joseph, 100 percent as human as we are, shows us the way.

FROM LIMITATIONS TO COMMUNION

> While they were there, the time came for her to deliver her child. And she gave birth to her firstborn son and wrapped him in bands of cloth, and laid him in a manger, because there was no place for them in the inn. (Luke 2:6–7)

> When the angels had left them and gone into heaven, the shepherds said to one another, "Let us go to Bethlehem and see this thing that has taken place, which the Lord has made known to us." So they went with haste and found Mary and Joseph, and the child lying in the manger. (Luke 2:15–16)

Popular devotion wanted to see the Holy Family going door to door looking for shelter, finding only refusal. It seems, however, inconceivable that those people from Bethlehem had a heart capable of leaving a woman in labor and her husband out in the open. It is also hard to imagine that the women of Bethlehem did not come close to Mary and assist her in childbirth. With great frequency, poor people are willing to share what they have, even if it is little.

No mother or father would wish their child to come into the world in poverty conditions. It is possible that Mary and Joseph would have prepared the best they had to welcome their child, within their modest means. But the delivery came in due course when nature marked its time, no one could overtake or stop it in an appropriate scenario. The circumstances changed the script in such a way that Mary ended up being forced to give birth in a crowded town, in which there was no other better place than a manger to lay down the newborn, a place to be warm and have a little space to breathe.

This situation could have caused deep pain in the heart of Joseph for at least two reasons. First of all, because love wishes to avoid all suffering of the loved one. Joseph loved Mary and he must have found it embarrassing to see her exposed to such a delivery after the long road they had just traveled. Second, Joseph might have felt discomfort to reach his limits and to discover he was unable to secure optimal conditions for his family. Maybe he thought he was not up to the mission he received. Perhaps his thoughts tormented him, considering that he should never have undertaken the trip.

When things do not come out as we have planned, our self-image is damaged. We question our capabilities and tend to experience a feeling of failure. Sometimes we blame something outside ourselves and on other occasions we blame ourselves. Ultimately, it is difficult to accept that reality does not bend to our designs.

The COVID-19 pandemic gave us a great lesson in this sense. There are serious events that happen without our own direct responsibility or that of others. Facing the evil that escapes our control, we have the option to lock ourselves up and bemoan it and focus on a cycle of negativity, without stopping. We can alternatively breathe deeply and set out an open plan that allows us to discover options never imagined.

The Evangelists do not tell us how Joseph immediately reacted, but we do know he was able to get back on the road when the angel ordered him to do so. We also know he was present when the shepherds came to worship Jesus. These things allow us to think that Joseph was able to accept a process of allowing the pain caused by experiencing poverty and its limitations to open him to the joy of new communion, knowing his own fragility and opening him to those who count the least in the world.

At that time, shepherds were marginalized because they lacked religious instruction and their way of life prevented them from fulfilling the law. They are visited by angels who announce great joy: not only "a Savior is born" but a Savior "to you" is born—precisely to them. They will recognize him by certain signs contrary to the world's glory: a child, some bands of cloth, a manger. The Messiah is revealed to the most marginalized social group.

Joseph witnesses the joy of the shepherds, who wanted to verify if the announcement was real and true. Joseph also contemplates these ordinary people whose testimony lacks value, yet they run out to announce their joy to everyone who wants to hear them. Joseph closes his eyes to savor this good news: the poor, the little ones, are the first announcers; salvation is for everyone, but it spreads from beneath.

If a census had not hindered the natural course of events, Jesus would probably have been born in Nazareth and the shepherds would not have found the child lying in a manger, poor just like them. When we are ready to let the light of the gospel enter our life, all poverty and all fractures become a place of grace. Fragility is revealed then as a privileged space for communion.

FROM MISUNDERSTANDING TO MEANING

> After eight days had passed, it was time to circumcise the child; and he was called Jesus, the name given by the angel before he was conceived in the womb. (Luke 2:21)

> She will bear a son, and you are to name him Jesus for he will save his people from their sins. (Matt 1:21)

The announcement of the birth of Jesus did not come accompanied with an instruction manual. The parents might be wondering with some concern what a creature would be like begotten by the Holy Spirit: would it have a normal body? Whom was he going to look like? How would he behave? Would he grow up as any other child? If the apocryphal Gospels cover the birth and childhood of Jesus like a mantle full of fantastic and rich details, the canonical narratives are very sober and leave only a glimpse of the first stage of the life of Jesus, which was developed following the common ways of all human beings.

A common life, even in the midst of painful and unusual circumstances, could provoke in Joseph the pain of not understanding anything. "How is it possible–he could tell Mary–that the Son of God depends totally on us, that he cries when he is hungry, not knowing how to talk or walk?" The days went by, without anything extraordinary happening and without receiving new guidance to allow them to understand what his wife and he himself are living.

And in this way, without understanding much, they arrive at the date on which the law of Moses prescribes circumcision for males: "At the eighth day the flesh of his foreskin shall be circumcised" (Lev 12:3). The circumcision expresses the belonging of the male to a covenant community dating back to Abraham. This covenant is irrevocable and marks indelibly the identity of the person, going through the man's deepest innermost self and the desire to keep the memory of his name:

> God said to Abraham, "As for you, you shall keep my covenant, you and your offspring after you throughout their generations. This is my covenant, which you shall keep, between me and you and your offspring after you: Every male among you shall be circumcised. You shall circumcise the flesh of your foreskins, and it shall be a sign of the covenant between me and you." (Gen 17:9–11)

Joseph has seen Jesus born under the laws of nature. Pregnancy, childbirth, and diapers are convincing signs of his true humanity. Now on the eighth day he himself must lead Jesus to meet for the first time the laws of his people, for circumcision will be the sign of his communion with the history and destiny of Israel. Joseph does not have—perhaps will never have—all the tools to understand that humanity is not unfamiliar to this child. In a circumstance of misunderstanding, surely a painful one, Joseph chooses to do "what he has to do," nothing more, and in this way he begins to open his innermost self to the deepest sense of history, which escapes his first glance.

At the circumcision ceremony, males receive their name. Although the Gospels do not note a single word from Joseph, it is he, as a father, who pronounces the name of his son. Joseph calls his newborn "Jesus" for two very precise reasons, because that is how the angel told him in dreams and because this child "will save his people from their sins." The mysterious reach of present events lies hidden in this name—God has become the people, God is with us, God saves. When closing his eyes once more, Joseph agrees to this project, which for the moment starts only with the cry of pain of the child being circumcised. Joseph's misunderstanding is not lost in irrationality or absurdity, but it plunges into the mystery and prepares him to embrace the internal coherence of each event, not at the time convenient for him but at the hour of God.

How many times we would like to remove the sense of reality, unable to bear the anguish of not understanding certain facts. With his attitude, Joseph indicates the path of historical patience, which does not avoid the risk of having to go on moving forward and taking blind decisions. But this helps to develop the capacity for standing by, ready. Patience sharpens the gaze when this frees the immediate concern. It is not necessary to understand everything that happens to us to surrender ourselves to every instant.

Sometimes we need to learn to consent to more docility relative to circumstances, to simply accept "what comes" and to do "what you have to do" without looking for an emergency exit or extraordinary trails. Sometimes it takes time, a long time, to discover with gratitude that God has always been present saving us from thorny situations and complicated relationships. And then, little by little, we begin to guess that it is there precisely, in the difficulties of life, where God meets us.

FROM APPREHENSION TO INTUITION

Then Simeon blessed them and said to his mother Mary, "This child is destined for the falling and the rising of many in Israel and to

> be a sign that will be opposed so that the inner thoughts of many will be revealed and a sword will pierce your own soul too." (Luke 2:34–35)

> Simeon took him in his arms and praised God saying, "Master, now you are dismissing your servant in peace, according to your word; for my eyes have seen your salvation, which you have prepared in the presence of all peoples, a light for revelation to the Gentiles and for glory to your people Israel." (Luke 2:28–32)

After the circumcision of Jesus, the days continue passing without new signs, until reaching the moment to fulfill two new precepts that Luke unifies in a single ceremony: the purification of Mary (cf. Lev 12:1–8) and the rescue of Jesus as the firstborn (cf. Num 18:15–16). On this occasion, Joseph and Mary meet Simeon in the temple: "This man was righteous and devout, looking forward to the consolation of Israel, and the Holy Spirit rested on him" (Luke 2:25).

It would not seem strange that the words of Simeon would have aroused in Joseph a movement of apprehension when he prophesies that Jesus will be a sign of contradiction for his people and that a sword of pain will pierce the soul of Mary. Before a defenseless newborn and before a young and full-of-life woman, it is difficult to interpret the mysterious meaning of these frightening words.

Once again, Joseph does not ask for explanations, but rather he listens and keeps everything in his heart. He does not question whether all the difficulties that they are going through—and the ones ahead—are worthy in view of an uncertain and painful panorama. Neither is he paralyzed by his restlessness. Maybe he closed his eyes for a moment to take a deep breath before discussing with his wife the "titles" Simeon has attributed to the Child: salvation for all peoples, light to illuminate the gentiles, the glory of Israel.

The experience of apprehension is often dreadful. While fear may refer to a real and immediate danger, apprehension is a threat diffused from certain malignity that can come upon us, and that even causes somatic symptoms such as insomnia or the feeling of having a knot in one's stomach. The shadow of the future often blurs the present moment and steals from us the energy we need here and now. Sometimes it happens that the complications so feared never come, and we give ourselves late awareness of having suffered uselessly. At other times, threats are in fact transformed into trouble, but when they arise, we have the necessary resources to face them. We often forget that grace is never given to us in advance.

When we get trapped in fear, it diminishes our ability to perceive other surroundings in the reality that can help us to interpret, and even to overcome, what is happening to us. Joseph does not easily deny the future risk that Simeon has just outlined, but he does not let himself be imprisoned by anxiety. His thoughts remain clear to remember and recognize that this Child, although he will later become a sign of contradiction for the world and a cause of suffering for his mother, will also be the salvation for all peoples. The light always makes its way through the dark, like the sentinel who awaits the dawn cannot doubt it in the middle of the night.

The intuition of life that emerges from the gloomier realities, far from dragging us into a sterile optimism, opens the door to a hopeful and creative realism. Simeon's prophecy penetrates the innermost being of Joseph. Instead of being blocked by the imminent shadows over Jesus, Joseph sets him on the present course of his life, whereby the salvation promised from the very beginning may come true in the future.

FROM UNCERTAINTY TO FREEDOM

> Now after they had left, an angel of the Lord appeared to Joseph in a dream and said, "Get up, take the child and his mother, and flee to Egypt, and remain there until I tell you; for Herod is about to search for the child, to destroy him." Then Joseph got up, took the child and his mother by night, and went to Egypt, and

> remained there until the death of Herod. This was to fulfill what had been spoken by the Lord through the prophet, "Out of Egypt I have called my son." (Matt 2:13–15)

When Joseph sees a crying child, perhaps he feels that God fills the world through unreliable means. However, he does not take time to please his intuitions or dreams right away. He rises and sets off for Egypt, taking his wife and a newborn with him to flee the threat of death:

> Even through Joseph's fears, God's will, his history, and his plan were at work. Joseph, then, teaches us that faith in God includes believing that he can work even through our fears, our frailties, and our weaknesses. He also teaches us that amid the tempests of life, we must never be afraid to let the Lord steer our course. At times, we want to be in complete control, yet God always sees the bigger picture. (Pope Francis, *Patris Corde* 2)

What is paradoxical about this image is that Joseph gives up the helm of his boat to God and at the same time he continues to guide his boat with a firm hand and without failing. In the midst of the storm, Joseph and God make a covenant to save the life of Jesus and, in this way, steer the history of salvation.

We ignore absolutely everything that could have happened on the way to Egypt, but it likely was not as pleasant as some apocryphal Gospels claim. According to the Pseudo-Matthew, one day Mary was tired and hungry: "Then the baby Jesus, who was resting, serene on his mother's lap, said to the palm tree: 'Tree, bow down and feed my mother with your fruits.' And to these words the palm tree inclined its top to Mary's feet" (Gospel of Pseudo-Matthew 20:2). More than these prodigies, of which Matthew and Luke have not preserved trace, the flight to Egypt would be marked by fear and abandonment.

Once they had reached their destination, however, perhaps Joseph found a place to settle in the flourishing Jewish community that inhabited cities like Alexandria. In any case, life seems to go on without fear for some time, until the angel gives the order to return to Palestine.

This first stage of a certain peace in Egypt must have also been a time of uncertainty. Nothing that happened there is relevant enough for the Evangelists to make the least comment. No extraordinary sign comes to confirm the identity of Jesus. He grows as any other child. Immersed in that life without a clue, Joseph cannot guess what will be the next chapter, nor does he know what the salvation is announced by the name of Jesus. Joseph respects the freedom of a God who continues communicating with him through the confusion of dreams and does not offer a clear sign of the divinity of Jesus.

This process implies for Joseph the pain of relinquishing his expectations. "Let God be God" is without a doubt one of the deepest gestures of worship that a human being is able to perform, surrendered before the greatness of the One whose plans he does not know. And that disposition is not acquired without pain, which is humble and sublime at the same time, to bow inwardly to the mystery and let it speak God's way. Learning to respect the freedom of that Other who is God presupposes one is letting go of the desire to possess him.

Jesus, the Child—with a capital letter—is a child, lowercase. Where there are no particular signs, Joseph is called to contemplate the Presence who transforms everything. In his trivial, vulnerable, and threatened existence, Joseph must believe that God is expressing his beauty, his strength, and his glory.

When we are tempted to reduce reality, relationships, and even ourselves to the narrow framework of our poor expectations, Joseph invites us to carry out a process that broadens the soul and that moves from uncertainty toward freedom. We have to let go of the moorings of everything that we would like to apprehend (our image, relationships, past successes, future projects...) to let life keep giving new possibilities of being and living in the world.

The COVID-19 pandemic showed us that reality is different from the best calculated plans. In a way, going through the uncertainty of that time, traced within us paths of a more authentic freedom. "Let be," as painful as it gets sometimes, will perhaps lead us to discover the joy of "letting ourselves be" who we really are without proving it and "letting God be" who he wants to be for each one of us.

FROM FEAR TO FULFILLMENT

> But when he heard that Archelaus was ruling over Judea in place of his father Herod, he was afraid to go there. And after being warned in a dream, he went away to the district of Galilee. There he made his home in a town called Nazareth, so that what had been spoken through the prophets might be fulfilled, "He will be called a Nazarene." (Matt 2:22–23)

Joseph's fourth and final dream narrated by Matthew contains an alarming new indication. The danger that motivated the flight to Egypt has not completely disappeared, so that the return to Palestine requires another good dose of prudence and audacity:

> God always finds a way to carry out his saving plan. So too, our lives may at times seem to be

> at the mercy of the powerful, but the Gospel shows us what counts. God always finds a way to save us, provided we show the same creative courage as the carpenter of Nazareth, who was able to turn a problem into a possibility by trusting always in divine providence. (Pope Francis, *Patris Corde* 5)

Joseph does not give into the temptation of letting a real threat—represented by Archelaus—block the fulfillment of God's project, even when it has been communicated in the middle of the confusion of dreams. His "creative courage" allows him to "transform a problem into an opportunity." Far from denying danger, Joseph identifies it and gives fear its rightful place, without giving it permission to take over and paralyze the future opening up before him.

Fear is one of the basic emotions of any human being, also shared by the rest of the mammals. Although it causes unpleasant sensations, fear itself is not negative. By putting ourselves on guard against existing risks, it helps us to survive. It only becomes a problem when we manage poorly, granting it the power to dominate our thoughts and actions.

"What would I do if I was not afraid?" If we honestly consider this question, we may be surprised to see certain gaps between our deep desires and concrete decisions we are making and between those and the structure of our life. The fear of losing security or taking a chance on uncertain adventures can frustrate the growth of the most genuine core in us, of what our heart really wants. If we believe that the will of God is expressed in authentic desires, fear can prevent us from living according to God's dream.

Many times Joseph must have experienced this all-too-human emotion that is fear. We do not know how he handled it personally, but we know the actions he performed. When he learns that a son of Herod is reigning in Judea, he decides not to stay in Egypt for fear that the new sovereign could find Jesus. But he does not act with recklessness by returning to Judea and unnecessarily exposing his family to danger. Instead of backing away in fear, Joseph listens to the message and takes advantage of it to start the process of fulfillment, perhaps different from what he had planned: "He went to live in a city called Nazareth." Remember that the Evangelist Matthew omits the episode of the annunciation to Mary and the journey from Nazareth to Bethlehem on the occasion of the census.

"If at times God seems not to help us, surely this does not mean that we have been abandoned, but instead are being trusted to plan, to be creative, and to find solutions ourselves" (Pope Francis, *Patris Corde* 5). Trust in God support us and enables us to support ourselves in him, and also to seek in ourselves and among us all the resources that can help us in clearing certain complicated horizons. It is not foolish to imagine that Joseph would talk to Mary and together they would decide what was the best way and share the responsibility of possibly being wrong.

Breaking out of fear and opening up destabilizing possibilities is a hurried exercise that demands trust, generosity, courage...and a little bit of humor. Although it sometimes seems impossible, Joseph shows that this task is within our reach when we use all our creativity and, at the same time, count on some intercessions while holding onto God's providence. The pain of fear then makes way for the joy of recognizing the fulfillment of God's plans—placed in our innermost desires—through simple fruits that generate abundant life.

FROM ABSENCE TO ENCOUNTER

> And when he [Jesus] was twelve years old, they went up as usual for the festival. When the festival had ended and they started to return, the boy Jesus stayed behind in Jerusalem, but his parents did not know it. Assuming that he was in the group of travelers, they went a day's journey. Then they started to look for him among their relatives and friends. When they did not find him, they returned to Jerusalem to search for him. After three days they found him in the

> temple, sitting among the teachers, listening to them and asking them questions. And all who heard him were amazed at his understanding and his answers. (Luke 2:42–47)

The scriptures are full of experiences of loss that give a good reason for the absence of spiritual life:

> Upon my bed at night I sought him whom my soul loves; I sought him, but found him not; I called him, but he gave no answer. "I will rise now and go about the city, in the streets and in the squares; I will seek him whom my soul loves." I sought him but found him not. (Song 3:1–2)

> Early on the first day of the week, while it was still dark, Mary Magdalene came to the tomb.... They have taken away my Lord, and I do not know where they have laid him. (John 20:1, 13)

Authentic love, by its very nature, does not hold onto the one being loved but rejoices in the beloved's freedom, so that the lover endures the risk of losing the beloved and triggers a searching dynamic. But our love tends frequently to lock in the beloved after having found him/her. Perhaps that is why Jesus tells Mary Magdalene, "Do no hold on to me, because I have not yet ascended to the Father" (John 20:17).

Joseph lives the experience of losing Jesus. Luke claims that for three days he and Mary searched for him "anguished." At the time this scene occurs, Jesus is twelve years old and nothing shows that extraordinary events might occur in his existence: he grows, progresses, and learns. Joseph has been loving this child more and more, this child who grows like every child in Nazareth, and perhaps he is finally enjoying the relative calm of living a normal life under the shelter of a family and a community. He probably is teaching Jesus his own work, to prepare him to start fulfilling all the precepts of the law for the day when he will be thirteen years old.

The episode at the temple marks a new pain for Joseph, not only because he and Mary physically lose sight of Jesus for three days, but also because when finding him among the doctors, their son is no longer exactly the same as he was in Nazareth. In Jerusalem, Jesus lives a particular experience that makes him progress in revealing his identity. This does not mean that at this moment Jesus acquires a full awareness of his divine sonship and mission, which would deny his true humanity. Human beings—and Jesus is one—are discovering our identity progressively, without ever reaching a full grasp of our own mystery.

Jesus will try, without success, to explain to Mary and Joseph what he is living: "He said to them, 'Why were you searching for me? Did you not know that I must be in my Father's house?' But they did not understand what he said to them" (Luke 2:49-50). The parents of Jesus are suddenly seen excluded from a very special intimacy—that of Jesus and his Abba—in which they do not directly participate. This new form of absence is perhaps even more painful than the first one: the lost child can be found on his own, but this Child whom they begin to lose, takes with him the few certainties and expectations they have been able to conceive until now.

Like Mary Magdalene at the feet of the Risen Lord, Joseph and Mary are called not to hold onto this Jesus who begins his own adult life. But Jesus, instead of telling them not to stop him, "went down with them and came to Nazareth and was obedient to them" (Luke 2:51). Jesus goes on discovering for many years "the things of his Father" immersed in the irrelevance of Nazareth. Joseph sees how he becomes a craftsman like him, although in his mind he has registered certain signs that allow him to think his son's fate will not be the same as all the other boys of the town. Joseph has to live a new process from the disconcerting absence that generates the growth of Jesus. This son whose mystery exceeds him, leads Joseph toward the deep joy from the believing encounter.

Perhaps Joseph will close his eyes many times to contemplate deep down in his heart the chapters of the history of Jesus that they have lived together, the history that is written so slowly, and to remember the confusing voice that spoke to him long ago in dreams. When he opens his eyes again, Joseph will perhaps have the intuition with joy and amazement to see the Son of God in the son of Mary, the Word made Nazarene.

MIRACLES

Everyday life, in its simplicity, is a fertile ground where extraordinary things occur that are necessary to discern with the eyes of faith. The great believers are characterized by their ability to discover the presence of God where others only manage to stay on the surface of events. Elijah, at Horeb, discovers the delicate presence of God in a gentle breeze where for others maybe it would not represent more than a brief relief on a hot summer afternoon.

In Nazareth, Mary and Joseph were nourished by faith. Living day by day with Jesus, whose existence runs along with the currents of his contemporaries, they do not see in him any wonder to confirm the messages received before his birth. Mary and Joseph deeply believe in placing their unconditional trust in the God of Israel who leads them to approach the dark and long years of Jesus.

In the Fourth Gospel, John recounts seven miracles of Jesus under the name of "signs." If we stop to contemplate the figure of Joseph in the light of Scripture, we can discover in it also seven signs that propose a concrete way to face daily life, overflowing all limits and forecasts. But before we get into these "seven miracles of Joseph," we should clarify our understanding a *miracle*.

First of all, a miracle is an extraordinary event. It is something out of the ordinary and the expected, not for showing off but for relinking human beings with God, as a reminder of our dependence on the Creator and his call to live in covenant. Therefore, a miracle does not aim to make a show of divine force to dazzle human beings, but rather it is a sign of God's tenderness—his power to love beyond all limits.

As a consequence, a miracle is above all good news, an announcement that God takes over from reality and comes to redeem what is happening. We could say, in summary, that a miracle causes a widening in reality so that it reaches further from where it could reach by itself.

The reference of every miracle is Jesus: his person, his words, his actions; he is the definitive intervention of God in history. All of his life is an announcement of the kingdom that is to come, from the first moment of his conception, through the years of his ordinary life in Nazareth and his preaching on the roads of Galilee, up to the paschal events. Jesus is "the miracle of the Father." He shows us with wholeness who God is. Therefore, any other miracle will have to make direct reference to Jesus and the gospel.

Can we then properly speak of "the miracles of Joseph," if we take into account that the Evangelists do not relate any prodigies performed by him? Pope Francis does not suggest this surprising question but dares to go even further. "Joseph was the man chosen by God to guide the beginnings of the history of redemption. He was the true 'miracle' by which God saves the child and his mother" (Pope Francis, *Patris Corde* 5). From the pope's writings, let us contemplate Joseph's "seven miracles."

LISTENING

Matthew narrates the four dreams of Joseph: the annunciation, the flight to Egypt, the return to Israel, and his establishment in Galilee. Otherwise, none of the Evangelists say that Joseph had communicated directly with God. Through dreams, Matthew inserts Joseph in the line of the patriarchs and prophets, all of them great interlocutors of God throughout the history of salvation.

This dream language is not new to the biblical narratives. Abraham receives "in a deep sleep" the promise of the covenant (cf. Gen 15:12–16). Asleep at Bethel, Jacob hears from Yahweh the promise of the land and offspring (cf. Gen 28:10–19). Jeremiah describes another dream:

> Yahweh Sabaoth, the God of Israel, says this, "In the country of Judah and its towns, they will use these words once more, when I bring their captives home: Yahweh bless you, home of saving justice, holy mountain! And in this country, Judah and all its towns, the peasants and those who wander with their flocks, will live together, for I shall give the weary all they need and satisfy all those whose strength has gone" At this, I awoke and saw that my sleep had been sweet to me. (Jer 31:23–26)

Dreams, in their complexity, are a good metaphor of human communication. We all know from experience that communicating is a difficult exercise, because we can't always express what we want to say, and we do not always get to listen and understand the other. As much as we try, communication is not transparent; in the dialogue there always remains a trace of uncertainty. How do we listen deeply when the mystery of the other can escape us?

This is where the miracle begins, because Joseph is a master of the difficult art of listening. He does not set the conditions for the dialogue to make it possible. He simply accepts the word addressed to him in given circumstances. He does not make excuses "pretending to be asleep," as if the word were not addressed to him. In the middle of the interferences and confusion within the dreams, Joseph listens with his whole being and embraces God's plans.

Matthew does not say that Joseph's reply to the angel of God was in words. Joseph answers with his actions, with his decisions. His listening is active and responsible, which is translated into the ability to be set aside and to change his own plans, to go places he would not have chosen and take charge of completely unexpected situations.

BELIEVING

Dreams are finished and life goes on. Imagine how Joseph had to rub his eyes to know if what he had dreamed was true. Let us imagine how his heart vibrated in receiving the words addressed to him... and upon waking, Joseph "believed" the dream and prepared for traveling to fulfill the mission he received from God via the angel.

Sometimes we think that believing is the same as professing a series of rites, like going to church or saying prayers. Without a doubt, such acts and many others are expressions of faith, and faith is nurtured by them. But believing goes far beyond devotion.

Faith is a force that moves the entire person. It does not affect only one area of our being (the head, ideas, sensibility, will, actions), nor even a portion of our time. We cannot be a believer only on Sunday when we go to Mass or when we volunteer to do something for others, or just be a personal believer when we pray in private.

Let's pause for a moment to consider the image we have of what a good believer is. There are many wrong representations: a true believer does not have to be someone who has studied a lot of theology or who receives special visions and spends so much time in church. Let us rather think, with Pope Francis, about so many "saints next door" who listen to the word of God and put it into practice without regard for obstacles, all the while living daily life.

Joseph is a teacher of faith because he lives in the depth of its essential dimensions. He believes that the word given to him is true. He gives recognition to God through the angel's intercession. Abandoning himself to God, he embraces with all his being the divine will, without knowing where this is going to lead him.

Joseph understands that believing is acting: "For just as the body without the spirit is dead, so faith without works is also dead" (Jas 2:26). Joseph "did as the angel of the Lord commanded him and took her as his wife" (Matt 1:24). First, Joseph listens and then he gives a concrete answer as committed believer. He does what he is told, he executes the mission entrusted to him. Joseph does not fabricate his mission, he does not negotiate with God. He acts faithfully, specifically on the order he receives, although he knows this is going to complicate his life. He assumes the change of plans and allows the reins of his own life to be carried by others. He lets himself be guided by the whisper of his heart. He surrenders to God's project without making calculations or bargains.

TRUSTING

Trust is an essential aspect of faith. In Hebrew, the word *believe* involves a safety dimension and stability born from the certainty of being supported by someone and abandoning oneself to him. "If you do not stand firm in faith, you shall not stand at all" (Isa 7:9). Psalm 146:5 portrays the believer as he "whose hope is in the Lord."

Trust, as communication, is a very difficult human exercise, and it is built from childhood. An adult will have more ability to trust if during the first years of life he has felt secure, taken care of and in good hands. Confidence is shaped from positive experiences of being supported by others, who will be there for us in good or bad situations, whatever happens.

However, usually our trust is wounded, not only because we carry the impression of certain bad experiences lived in childhood, but also because during adult relationships we go through disappointments and disagreements. We thought that a person was a true friend...and just when we most needed him, we realize we cannot count on him. We thought we were well considered at work...then next day they dismiss us or early retire us. Who else has experienced similar scenarios, which are part of a normal life?

Faced with these painful experiences that hurt our confidence, we can harden and shut down to avoid being attacked again. Self-protection is most basic: how many people do not even speak to each other within families? How many friendships are broken? Sometimes it seems that in order to recover certain situations it requires a true miracle.

And here Joseph returns with a word to tell us or, better, with an attitude to show us—an image worth more than a thousand words. Joseph listens to God and depends completely on him. He lets his stability rest on a voice he has heard in dreams. What insecurity! But because he has truly listened and believed, Joseph places his confidence in the Lord with the certainty that he will not be abandoned.

Joseph is a trusted teacher because he does not only trust in God but also in Mary. God helps those who help themselves, says a common proverb. Deep down, trust in God that does not take steps toward trusting others seems suspicious. Joseph trusts Mary, relying on the word from the angel and also on Mary's word. What uncertain words they are: those of the angel and a word received in dreams! Mary's is the word of a woman and is of no value in Jewish society, which is why a woman could not testify in a trial. Joseph is motivated by two fragile words, the angel's and Mary's, yet he trusts entirely and unconditionally.

Joseph's trust has several "miraculous effects." The first one is to save Mary from stoning, which was the fate of an adulterous woman in a Jewish community. Before receiving the word from the angel, Joseph had decided to dismiss Mary quietly. Though not understanding, he believed in Mary's innocence and thought of abandoning her to save her from a certain and shameful death. Matthew says that Joseph was a just man. In the biblical sense of *justice*, this does not mean to give each one what corresponds or belongs to him, but rather to be in favor of the weakest.

The second miraculous effect of Joseph's confidence is to allow God to carry out the divine project freely, thanks to the gift of a human father for his Son. Joseph becomes the legal father of Jesus, an essential figure for the Jewish world. Through Joseph, Jesus finds a place in the Israelite community, receives education in the faith, and acquires an occupation to make his living. As a father, Joseph embodies for Jesus during his early years the face of his heavenly Father: the expression *abba*, so dear to Jesus, would be taught by Mary to address Joseph. Joseph represents the male role model for Jesus: like father, like son. During his public life, Jesus is a man who values women and knows how to relate to everyone. We might think that since Joseph was Jesus' model in childhood and youth, both were alike.

And the third wonder is that Joseph's confidence becomes a source of stability, of trust for Mary and for Jesus. Joseph, who has entirely trusted in God and in Mary, becomes a solid and safe pillar, not just for a woman still in her teens and for the Child about to be born, but for the whole history of salvation. Thanks to Joseph's trust, God's loving plan is accomplished through a complex itinerary full of adversity.

STARTING AGAIN

Among the traditional representations of Joseph, there are certain depictions that present him on a trip: the arrival to Bethlehem, the flight to Egypt, the return to Nazareth. These passages tell us about a fourth miracle of Joseph, the miracle of starting all over again.

In life we start getting tired. When we are young, we think we could conquer the world. This is wonderful, because thanks to this energy, we can give ourselves entirely to a goal that we are passionate about. But the time of great ideals does not last forever and little by little we start to slow down. Sometimes it is a frustration or a disappointment that tells us that the relationship is not worth it. Other times, it is the difficulty of everyday life or the growing need for tranquility and peace. Without realizing it, we are setting our own area of comfort and it is more difficult for us to be available to respond to our destiny.

There are situations that dramatically take us out from the tranquility acquired: an illness, a dismissal, the death of a loved one, an accident, a marriage breakdown, a vocational crisis. In these scenarios, it seems that the world is caving in on us. We have no choice but to start over, and how difficult it is!

Starting over is scary, it awakens many ghosts. What if I don't have the strength? What if I stay lying in the road? What if there is no one by my side to help me? So many "what ifs..." paralyze and overwhelm us.

Joseph lives this very human experience in himself. His life, as later will be true of the life of Jesus, is not linear, but is full of curves, comings and goings, and turns. Like ours! The first great shake-up for Joseph is the news of knowing that Mary is pregnant. This will force him to make other plans, taking on a son who is not his but doing so as if he were. What a spirit so great, so generous, is that of Joseph.

But with this confusion of plans, history has only just begun. Shortly after making his decision to welcome Mary into his home, he has to depart to Bethlehem to fulfill a citizenship obligation: the census. They all went, Joseph too, taking with him a woman in the last days before delivering her baby. Faith and trust do not avoid anguish. Imagine Joseph's concern if the delivery is sooner or complicated during the travel of more than 93 miles on foot.

After the Child's successful birth, and once the census procedures are fulfilled, Joseph receives—in a dream—a warning from the angel to flee to Egypt because Herod is looking for the Child to kill him. Egypt is not right next door. Again Joseph has to change plans, save the lives of Jesus and Mary, accept emigration, look for a way to reach such a destination, and find a way to survive there in an unknown land.

What comes later is another change of direction when the angel tells him to go back to Israel. So Joseph takes the Child and his mother and sets off again, ready to rebuild life in his homeland. Joseph could have been tired, he could have said, "Once is fine and twice, well okay, but three or four is too many already! We stay in Egypt!" However, he listens, believes, and trusts, and in that trust he finds the strength to start all over again.

Pilgrim Joseph, always called to start again, always ready to start over, can inspire each of us in the twists and turns of our way. Special attention is needed for people who, like him, are forced to abandon their country and their family: the refugees, whose life is literally in danger; or economic migrants, who leave all in search of a better future for themselves and their children. In our fragmented society, where most people are inclined to do their own thing, to always start all over again, despite the tiredness of life, seems indeed a real miracle.

CARING WITHOUT APPROPRIATING

Joseph receives a unique mission in the history of salvation, which is to bring up the Son of God. It is a tremendous responsibility that falls suddenly on his shoulders, and it would scare anyone. We don't know how Joseph lived this mission or what questions he would ask through the years, as he saw Jesus grow up and nothing special was happening.

There is, however, one clue we can follow: the one Luke leaves us in the story of the ascent to Jerusalem when Jesus reached puberty. At thirteen years of age, the Jewish male reaches the legal age of majority; therefore, at age twelve, Jesus was already preparing for it. Mary and Joseph had cared for him until then. But that day, on the way back from the pilgrimage, they lose sight of him. (Remember that it was a caravan in which the relatives and friends of the town traveled together.) At age twelve, Jesus was already left with enough autonomy to walk alone among his people; his parents trusted him, they cared without overprotecting him, they were not possessive.

We can secretly suspect that Joseph and Mary "were overconfident," showing even a little irresponsibility. Yet, how do you allow an adolescent to have his own experiences if you tend to avoid all dangers? Joseph accepts the risk, and this is going to give him a huge fright.

Joseph allows Jesus to grow "in stature, wisdom and grace," as Luke says. He does not force him to go faster than he can. He does not impose a model, but he also does not stop him in his discoveries or in his searching. Joseph allows Jesus to come little by little into his own autonomy, to have human and spiritual experiences that gradually shape his humanity. Joseph is a model of identification for Jesus, but he does not pretend that Jesus is a copy of himself—he lets him be, to seek and express himself. He accompanies him in his growth, leaving him free, without holding him back.

The task of education is very complex and arduous. It is difficult to let the other be himself and go his own way, even to make his own mistakes. On the one hand, we tend to lead others where we think they should go to make it easier for them. On the other hand, how difficult it is to take care of those who have been entrusted to us without being their masters and commanders! How much jealousy and quarrels have arisen in any human group, how many rigidities and misunderstandings, for wishing to appropriate this task to ourselves?

Joseph, with his manner of educating Jesus, inspires us in a way of caring for people, accompanying them to perform tasks and putting their good and personal growth ahead of our personal safety and satisfaction.

LIVING IN THIRD PLACE

When Mary and Joseph finally find Jesus sitting among the teachers and arguing with them, the one who speaks first is Mary, a woman. This scene is amazing. In the ancient Jewish world, a woman had no right to speak in public, even less in the presence of her husband, who represents the authority of the family. Joseph lets Mary take the initiative, he does not rebuke her, neither does he take away her word. He does not even react as he is being humiliated in his virility and authority. He knows who he is and what his place is; he assumes it with peace, without trying to occupy another position that is not his.

Joseph's position is difficult, and nobody wants it. The gold and silver medals have great value, but the bronze medal already seems to be over. However, the third place, a dark and irrelevant one, without obvious importance, is meant to be for us. A place not to be seen or to shine, where everything matters little.

We spend most of our lives in this third place, and sometimes we are against it! It makes us angry with others because we are not taken sufficiently into account by them. It bothers us when no one notices what we do with so much effort. It hurts us that they do not recognize our work or our good works enough. We feel humiliated when someone younger, or more educated, or friendlier overtakes us.

All this is deeply human and occurs daily at home, at work, in the community...we are made of this clay! We want to live freely but do not always want to pay the price, or we prefer others to pay for us.

The figure of Joseph is deeply inspiring to those who want to live in an integrated and unified way, in the position one has been given in life. Joseph teaches us the greatness of letting others go ahead of us without feeling humiliated or put aside:

> Each of us can discover in Joseph—the man who goes unnoticed, a daily, discreet, and hidden presence—an intercessor, a support, and a guide in times of trouble. Saint Joseph reminds us that those who appear hidden or in the shadows can play an incomparable role in the history of salvation. (Pope Francis, *Patris Corde*, Introduction)

Joseph shows us that a valuable person is the one who knows how to value others by assuming a third place, like him. This allow us to live our life with relief, without giving in to the temptation to feel the presence of others as a threat.

LEAVING IN SILENCE

According to the canonical Gospels, Joseph's trace is lost after the pilgrimage to Jerusalem. Luke states that Jesus went down with Mary and Joseph to Nazareth and lived under their authority. How long did Joseph live? Was he present at the baptism of Jesus? Did he accompany him during his public ministry? What did he die of? We know nothing.

The apocryphal Gospels were attempts to fill in the information void surrounding Jesus and his family. One of these narratives is "The History of Joseph the Carpenter," a Coptic text composed between the fifth and seventh centuries, in which Jesus personally narrates the life and death of Joseph. According to this account, Joseph lived 111 years and died in the company of Mary and Jesus. From this narrative, a rich iconography developed about the death of Joseph, which does not have biblical basis. This story also prompted the creation of the image of Joseph as protector of the dying. Surely he who at the time of his own death was accompanied by Jesus, who is Life, will know without a doubt how to help believers take the great final step.

Far beyond these apocryphal details, it turns out that the truly exciting and almost miraculous fact is that Joseph played a role in history and then withdrew from it the same way he lived: without noise, without leaving footprints, and in silence. In this way, Joseph shows us that to be a great believer, a key player in the history of salvation, you do not need to earn an award in the *Guinness World Records*, have great achievements to your name, or die in a particular and glorious way.

The only necessity is to live day by day with depth: listen, believe, trust, start all over again, care without appropriating, and take third place...and then leave without noise.

Living in this way, Joseph underlines our true reality as creatures. Deep down, and as long as we pretend to be the best, we are nothing more than "useless servants" in God's work, instruments in his hands that are always necessary and never essential.

Living like Jesus, experiencing life as he did in third place, is a true grace for oneself and for people around us. In a world where everything invites us to be consumed by self-interest, to shine and excel, to live like Joseph "being dark on earth, like a traveler in the night"...is it not a true miracle?